PRODUCT LAUNCH 360°

Requisites of Launching a
Product across the Globe.

Doctor TA Srinivasen

INDIA · SINGAPORE · MALAYSIA

Notion Press

No.8, 3rd Cross Street,
CIT Colony, Mylapore,
Chennai, Tamil Nadu – 600004

First Published by Notion Press 2021
Copyright © Doctor TA Srinivasen 2021
All Rights Reserved.

ISBN 978-1-63781-592-2

This book has been published with all efforts taken to make the material error-free after the consent of the author. However, the author and the publisher do not assume and hereby disclaim any liability to any party for any loss, damage, or disruption caused by errors or omissions, whether such errors or omissions result from negligence, accident, or any other cause.

While every effort has been made to avoid any mistake or omission, this publication is being sold on the condition and understanding that neither the author nor the publishers or printers would be liable in any manner to any person by reason of any mistake or omission in this publication or for any action taken or omitted to be taken or advice rendered or accepted on the basis of this work. For any defect in printing or binding the publishers will be liable only to replace the defective copy by another copy of this work then available.

Disclaimer

The publisher and the author makes
no representation or warranties with
respect to the completeness of the contents
of this work and specifically disclaim all warranties.
The information contained herein are indicative and
may differ from each and every geography across globe.
So necessary care and attention needs to be taken to
collate such requirements and comply with the same.

Dedication

The Author takes pride and pleasure in dedicating this book to young "*would be entrepreneurs*" across the world. It has been a struggle to have one source of reference on **360° pre-requisites** before a launch of product/services. This book is expected to give clarity on such essentials to entrepreneurs to spear head in their journey of product launch across the globe. The purpose of the book will be fulfilled if it really helps these budding entrepreneurs in avoiding possible pitfalls, take informed risks in launching of their product successfully.

CONTENTS

	Foreword	*9*
	Acknowledgements	*11*
1.	**Launch of New Product/Services** *Need for Compliance Plan*	13
2.	**Pricing of the Product** *Need and Strategies*	20
3.	**Sourcing of the Product** *Sourcing Models*	33
4.	**IPR Compliances** *Need for Proactive Steps*	39
5.	**Other Critical Factors** *Test Marketing* *Product Claims* *Legal Metrology Compliance* *Storing Related Compliance* *Usage Instructions* *Consumer Activism*	61

6.	**Risks - Product Launch & After** *Risk Mitigation through Insurance*	73
7.	**Compliance Requirements** *Need for a Comprehensive Check List*	109
	Indicative Task Responsibility Chart	*112*
	About The Author	*115*

FOREWORD

The Author of the book Product Launch 360°, **TA Srinivasen** is known to me from the time he was associated with CavinKare, as Group Head – Legal & Secretarial.

Product Launch 360° is the first-of-its-kind book that captures the pre-requisites essential for a successful launch of a product/services across the globe by an entrepreneur.

Launching a product requires various proactive steps to be undertaken and also to comply with various requirements prevalent in the geography before placing the same in the market by an entrepreneur. The author has succinctly brought out the same for the benefit of budding entrepreneurs, product managers including industries to comply with the same to avoid unnecessary hassles in the product launch and thereafter.

There are several books available on the modalities of product launch, but there is almost none that addresses the pre-requisites that need to be complied with, preceding a formal product launch. This book bridges the gap and fulfils the same.

The author with his solid academic background, qualitative experience, and accomplishments is the right person to come out with this book, which delineates the pre-requisites for a successful product launch. I am sure this book will prove to be a good reference in complying with the same.

It is my pleasure to affix this foreword to the book titled 'Product Launch 360°' and congratulate Doctor TA Srinivasen for the same.

Through this, I take the opportunity to request readers to use the information provided herein to make themselves as a Compliant Organization. This will go a long way in focussing their energies for the benefit of the consumers without any disruption on the product launch.

I wish this publication a great success.

C.K. Ranganathan
Founder Promoter & CMD, CavinKare Group
Republic Day the 26th January 2021, Chennai

ACKNOWLEDGMENTS

The author at the outset wishes to acknowledge Notion Press Publishing for their support and resources to complete this book.

The author is deeply grateful to his family members, his better half Maghalekshmi, Children Vishnupriya, Bharat and Son-in-law Rakesh for their love, support and co-operation.

The author is indebted to his late parents Audiyappan and Sundaravalli for their selfless sacrifice in his upbringing.

He is also, thankful to all the Promoters and Management of various Corporate Companies he was associated with for the last over three decades, which helped him to shape as an able Corporate Legal Counsel. The author also expresses his thanks and gratitude to Mr. C K Ranganathan, Chairman and Managing Director of CavinKare Group, Chennai for his forward.

The author craves and seeks the blessings of his family deity Arulmihu Sri Achiramavalli Amman, Anbil, Tiruchirappalli.

CHAPTER ONE

LAUNCH OF NEW PRODUCT/ SERVICES

Need for Compliance Plan

Every Inventor or any one with business acumen would desire to be an entrepreneur to produce and launch their Goods/Services to the Society within the Geography they operate upon. These budding entrepreneurs always have a burning desire to launch their dream product. Many people with an entrepreneurial bent of mind always would like to emulate the successful entrepreneurs and follow their footsteps. Some of them have the necessary wherewithal to offer value for money products, which may deliver much better results than that of other similar products available in the market. It is so unfortunate that these budding entrepreneurs does not have mentors in moving forward with their vision of launching their dream product. Each and every country requires entrepreneurs who based on their innate skill must be encouraged to produce products which delivers best results at an affordable costs. Their product should aim to bring consumer delight through their product usage. Across the world we observe many path breaking initiatives have been done by new entrepreneurs who have innovated in producing superior products which lead to raising the standards of living of people. Such novel initiatives usually comes from these first generation entrepreneurs, endowed with an *out of box* thinking. They do not get the much needed support from successful predecessor entrepreneurs, who can lead them by giving a **360° insight** of requirements necessary in launching their maiden product. Many of them cannot kick start due to the reason there is no information available on how to proceed in furtherance of their goal. Today Business, Industry and Commerce across the world are not separated by boundaries and all these budding entrepreneurs can make best use of this opportunity in launching their dream product in a wide market.

The clarity on the launch of the product can be achieved only when the possible route map is known to them to handle various issues that they may confront before the product launch journey and immediately thereafter. Commercial launch of a product is preceded by compliance of various factors, overcoming several bottlenecks, to sustain and be successful.

There are various factors that drives the success of a product, these factors include:

(a) Affordable Price:

The product must be affordable by all sections of the society. This may be possible by using the right inputs and break through Research and Development efforts. If the manufacturing costs comes down through cost management without compromising on quality, with lower price tag may give more affordability to the consumers to buy the product. The product pricing therefore cannot be higher than the competitive product available in the market unless the same really justifies.

(b) Superior Product Quality:

The product must be of superior quality for the cost incurred by a consumer. It should be definitely better than comparable products available in the market for the price paid by a consumer.

(c) Differentiator:

The product must tend to be a differentiator comparable with other identical products available in the market. The consumer must be in a position to easily differentiate the product from other products based on its beneficial features. This differentiator drives the success of a product.

(d) Environment Friendly:

The production and usage of the product must be environment friendly and should not harm the nature. This factor helps certain category of consumers to have better acceptability.

(e) Government recognition:

The product should not be in the negative list of the Government. If the product has wider Government recognition, it may promote wider acceptance among consumers, leading to success.

(f) Consumer friendly:

The product must be consumer friendly, if not it may lack acceptability.

(g) Uniqueness:

The product must have some uncommon characteristics and must be unique in its placement.

(h) Product Convenience:

The product must be easily available and purchased with less effort. In convenience to buy causes displeasure and may make consumers to switch over to other products.

(i) Multiple Usage:

If the product is capable of multiple usage with identical product delivery it may command much more acceptability.

(j) No side effects:

The product usage should give rise to side effects or any sort of complications over their body to anyone.

(k) Product Efficiency:

The product must have the efficiency for what it was intended. Non-efficiency may make acceptability difficult.

(l) Solution to an issue:

The product must give a solution to an issue confronted by a consumer. This aspect plays a key role in today's world.

(m) Noticeability:

The product must be noticeable both in off-line and online. This goes a long way in the acceptability of the product.

(n) Accreditation:

If the product certification has been obtained from accredited bodies and laboratories, may improve consumer confidence to attract more consumers to opt for the product.

(o) Proof of Delivery:

The new product consumers should see for themselves the product delivery characteristics as it was intended. This by itself will drive acceptability.

(p) Recall:

The new product should be capable of recall by the consumers. This may be possible if most of the above features are present in the product.

(q) Meets Consumer expectation:

The new product should meet the expectations of the consumers in matching their needs.

Thus when one or more of the factors discussed above are factored inside a product then the same becomes acceptable to the consumer leading to success.

However the commercial success of a product has different dimensions. It is not limited to quality alone, it means a lot in managing various factors, before the product is put into commercial orbit successfully and to sustain the same.

Thus before embarking upon the exercise of launching a product, various aspects needs to be taken care before a formal commercial launch. This book makes an attempts to capture these aspects which needs to be adhered to and taken care scrupulously by both the new product launcher as well as existing producers. The various aspects of adherence in the launch of the product stated in this book is indicative.

A detailed Comprehensive Compliance Plan needs to be worked out keeping in mind the various factors discussed herein and all other factors as applicable in the respective Geography. There may other aspects which also needs to be considered, adhered based on the nature of the product and various regulatory requirements as may be applicable. Needless to mention that every geography may have diverse sets of dynamic statutory requirements in the launch of a product/services which needs to be captured and complied. Therefore based on compliance of basic pre-requisites the product/services must proceed for a formal commercial launch. If not the product launch might suffer from unnecessary hurdles, time delay and complications in the form of losses, penalty and other risks.

CHAPTER TWO

PRICING OF THE PRODUCT

Need and Strategies

Cost and Profit factors plays a crucial role in a launch of a product. After conceiving the product, for commercial purpose it is foremost necessary for an entrepreneur to find out the cost of making the product and the possible market price of the product vis-à-vis such similar competitive products available in the market. It may be necessary to prepare a Cost Sheet to evaluate the possible cost with allowable fluctuations in the cost of raw materials in the making of such product. It is necessary to capture all the cost details direct or indirect, operational, administrative costs, below the line sales promotion expenses, special sales drive costs and other incidental expenses that needs to be incurred. Only on capturing these details it will help to plan, control and know, the means of reducing the input costs by better sourcing, substitution of cost effective inputs, credit management and so on. Reduction of costs is instrumental in increasing the bottom line which has a correlation to the top line growth.

The basic cost sheet needs to be prepared in knowing the cost of producing the product/services.

A. DIRECT COST	xxxx	Subtotal	Total
Raw Materials	xxxx		
Labour	xxxx		
B. INDIRECT COST	xxxxx		
Power	xxxx		
Fuel			
Factory Expenses			
	xxxx		
COST OF GOODS MANUFACTURED		xxxxx	
C. OPERATING COST	xxxxx		
Selling Expenses			
Sales Promotional Activities			
Depreciation on Fixed Assets	xxxx		
Total Selling Expenses		xxxx	
D. ADMINISTRATION COSTS	xxxx		
Office Salaries			
Administration Expenses			
Tax & Duties	xxxx		
Misc. Expenses	xxxx		
Total Administrative Costs		xxxxx	
TOTAL OPERATING COST (A+B+C+D)			xxxx

By preparing the above Cost Sheet the total figure of total Operating Cost is arrived at. Thereafter depending on the indirect expenses, an addition of 5 to 10 percentile need to be added to the same to take care of the fluctuations and other unpredicted costs.

Thus after knowing the Operating Cost figures, it is necessary for an entrepreneur to fix his Sales Price or the Maximum Retail Price (MRP). The MRP of the product must be fixed after taking into account the following factors:

(a) MRP of such similar products in the market:

The price of the proposed product should hover around such similar products of that category. There cannot be a wide gap in the pricing. If the new product is priced high it may lack consumer acceptance leading to piling of unsold stocks at every point of sale, leading to expiry of the same putting the entrepreneur to losses.

(b) GST and other components of levy on the product:

All the tax incidence and other regulatory levies including the GST should be taken into account while determining the retail price. If this aspect is ignored there will be lesser realization of revenues in the product. Lesser realization leads to lower budgets for sales promotion and resultant lower sales volume.

(c) Net Proceeds that needs to be realized out of the product:

Every entrepreneur may have a targeted net realization of the product. The targeted net realization usually depends on the pricing of similar products in the market. So this needs to be taken into account while fixing the maximum retail price.

(d) Interest Cost and other financial charges:

While fixing the final retail price it may be necessary to take into account the interest cost and all other financial charges levied by the bank/financial institutions. Such costs needs to be considered for net realization and in fixation of the retail price.

(e) Income Tax:

Income tax is levied on the profits made by an entrepreneur. Thus a chunk of profit goes away as income tax. The Government in order to promote industries in backward areas may give Income Tax holiday which facilitates more profit retention. If more profits are realized then the same may be ploughed back to business for further expansion. This component also needs to be taken into account by an entrepreneur in the overall planning.

(f) Other costs:

Certain costs if overlooked will lead to reduction in net realization. It will be in the interest of the entrepreneur to be sensitive and meticulous in taking all such hidden costs into account, while arriving at the final retail price.

If the net realization is not attractive or if there is no or little scope to increase the MRP in comparison with such other allied product category in the market, **then it will be in the interest of the entrepreneur to rethink over the proposal or take corrective steps that may be necessary** before moving forward on the launch of the product.

In addition various other factors that needs to be kept in mind for price fixation includes:

(a) Easy availability of Raw Materials without any difficulty:

If the Raw Materials are not available near the production place, it may be necessary to source the same from far-off places. This will lead to increase in logistics cost, which needs to be borne in mind in the pricing.

(b) Stability in the cost of Raw Materials basis the past history:

It may be necessary to study the past history of Raw Material price trends and on that basis the cost needs to be built in. If the price trends are volatile care needs to be taken to factor the average in the cost based on the trends.

(c) Revision of MRP by looking at the past history prevalent in the trade:

The past history of the pricing trends prevalent in the Industry must be studied, as to whether the Industry is matured to accept revision in prices frequently. If not appropriate call needs to be taken on the same.

(d) No wariness for that line of product among the consumers:

If a line of product does not command the acceptance of consumers from new entrepreneurs, care needs to be taken to fix lower price and hedge the same later.

(e) No price controlling mechanism by the Government:

If the pricing of the new product is subject to control or likely to come under control by the regulatory authorities then this aspect also needs to be factored while fixing the price. If the product per-se comes under control price mechanism in that geography, then the regulatory requirements to that effect needs to be complied with.

(f) The regulating authorities does not have any loatheness over the product:

If the regulating authorities have any loatheness over the product then there could be resistance among the consumers, also which needs to be taken care while fixing the MRP.

(g) Possible substitutes in the long run:

If the product is likely to have some possible substitutes then care should be taken, in not locking the capital in fixed costs, which may likely to become obsolete in the near future. So this aspect also needs to be considered and higher pricing fixed for the product.

(h) Storage, Longevity of the product:

Storage longevity of the product may allow the product to stay long while lesser longevity may not allow to stay longer in the point of sales. This aspect need to be kept in mind while fixing the retail price. Frequent change of retail price may be possible for such products.

(i) Change of Technology:

If the product is subject to frequent technology shifts then it may be necessary to price it accordingly to make the best out of it.

The above said factors are only indicative, there may be other factors, which also needs to be borne in mind while pricing a product in a new product launch. In addition all regulatory requirements must be complied with as may be notified by the Government/Regulatory Authorities from time to time. It is simple that the pricing of the product should be based on justifiable product deliverables from the stand point of the entrepreneur as well as the consumer.

The following are some strategies adopted in pricing of a product:

Strategies in Pricing:

- **Cost plus pricing:**

As discussed above a product may be priced after arriving at the cost of the product adding there on the proposed margins. This is a simple fool proof pricing.

- **Competition above pricing:**

As a strategy to show a perceived superiority, the pricing of the product will be determined at a higher level than the similar products of the competition. This may be suitable to an already established entrepreneur who has more line of successful products and established reputation in the market. However care needs to be taken in pricing of a new product since consumer may not welcome high price for a new product from an entrepreneur.

- **Competition equivalent pricing:**

As the very name suggests the pricing of a new product will be priced at the levels of the competition. This pricing is based on the level playing field with competition.

- **Competition below pricing:**

This may be adopted to price a new product below the price levels of the competition for such similar product. As a strategy, pricing below the competition may help to wean away the consumers from the competition and help penetrate the market. But care needs to be taken to ensure the quality of the end product.

- **Discounted pricing:**

It refers to artificially increase the value of the pricing and impress upon the consumers that discount is given on its MRP, thereby enticing them to purchase the product. Selectively depending on the circumstances it may be used for a new product pricing.

- **Below Cost Pricing:**

Below Cost pricing is a risky pricing wherein the new product may be offered at a price lesser than the market cost. This pricing is strategically used to wean away consumers from the competition and after acceptance slowly increase the price of the product.

- **Differential pricing:**

This refers to differential pricing is different geographies. The product produced in one geography may be placed at a higher price while the same may be less in another geography.

- **Anchor pricing:**

Though this is similar to discount pricing, here the price of the product is given at a value less than the 'list price' in view of the product launch.

The pricing of a product may have one or more combinations of the aforesaid pricing as a strategy to penetrate, obtain consumer recognition and acceptance in the crowded market.

In short the pricing of the product/services should be inviting the consumer to buy the product by offering value added services better than similar products available in the market. In any case the pricing of the product, needs to be determined after taking all costs into account, keeping in mind the differentiating product delivery features and the competition.

Pricing Compliance under Competition Law:

The United Nations Conference in the year 1980, approved the multilateral agreement on Restrictive Business Practices on Competition Policy which came out with a framework, on the implementation of Competition/ Anti-trust Law for the control of anti-competitive practices across the member countries. These Multilaterally Agreed Equitable Principles and Rules were formulated with a view to achieve the following matters:

1. To ensure that the benefits arising from the simplification of tariffs and non-tariff barriers affecting world trade are not prevented or adversely achieved by restrictive trade practices, affecting trade in developing countries;

2. Achieving greater competence in international trade especially in developing countries, in line with national goals of economic, social development and existing economic structures viz.,

- Creation, promotion and protection of competition;
- Control of the concentration of capital and/or economic power;
- Promotion of innovation;

3. Promote and protect the economic/social welfare interests of consumers in all countries with special attention to developing countries;

4. Eradication of hindrances to trade and development which may emanate from the restrictive trade practices followed in all countries with focus on developing countries;

5. Implementation of the same in all member countries.

Thus the Competition Law as prevalent in many countries is outcome of the frame work provided by the United Nations. The Law contains various provisions on pricing which need to be adhered in the pricing of the product.

The Competition Law generally prohibits the following:

- Anti-competitive Agreement or practices that restricts free trading and competition.
- Abusive behaviour using the Dominant Position
- Combinations like Mergers and Acquisitions that threatens the process of competition.

Prohibition under Competition Law:

Competition Law prohibits practices as delineated above, therefore an entrepreneur should not indulge in the same before or after launching his product.

The following are such practices which are illegal under competition law as prevalent in various countries:

- Allocating themselves territories by dividing or sharing markets through resolute action between competitors.
- Control production and services with a view to exercise control over the market.
- Tie-up arrangements, forcing a consumer to buy another product along with the main product.
- Predatory pricing by selling a product or service below cost with a view to drive competitors out of the market.
- Resale price maintenance stipulating to sell goods only at listed prices.
- Disproportionate pricing taking advantage of lack of competition.
- Creating artificial demand in the market by limiting the production of goods or services.
- Directly or indirectly, imposing unfair or discriminatory condition which has an adverse effect on the consumer.
- Indulge in bid-rigging or collusive bidding to be successful in tender contracts.
- Refusal to deal, by placing restriction to whom the goods are to be sold.

- Exclusive distribution agreements, to promote only one reseller.
- Abuse of dominance through abuse of market power by affecting the competition.
- Discriminatory pricing by charging different prices for the same goods in different market segments.
- Indulging in practices resulting in denial of market access to its competitors.

The overall contents of competition law varies from one country to that of another. However the important cardinal principle is to safeguard the interests of the consumers and ensure entrepreneurs to compete freely in the market.

It is therefore the duty of an entrepreneur not to indulge in such practices over pricing, prohibited under the relevant competition/anti-trust law of the geography.

CHAPTER THREE

Sourcing of the Product

Sourcing Model - Determination

Determination of Sourcing Business Model plays an important role in producing the product based on various factors like Operational Capability, Bandwidth to Produce, Protection of IPRs, Revenue and Choice of Operations. Few of these models are discussed below. An entrepreneur may adopt one or more or combo of such models, meeting his requirements. Even before planning for sourcing requirements it may be prudent on the part of an entrepreneur to ensure compliance of other aspects stated elsewhere in this book. This may prevent him from possible road blocks and support him against losses, in the journey of launching a product.

(a) Own Manufacturing:

An entrepreneur while launching a product may set up his own manufacturing unit to produce the product. This involves lot of planning, implementation, capital cost, time, wherewithal, energy, management and compliance to various legislations, rules and regulations. Due to the cost and complications in the manufacturing process many entrepreneurs turn to third party outsourcing of their products. This scope of this book is on the launch of the product from commercial point of view and therefore manufacturing issues are not focussed here.

(b) Third Party Outsourcing Model:

These days many entrepreneurs who own the brand and formulation adopt the model of Third Party Outsourcing of their products. Before deciding on the model it may be necessary to understand the merits and demerits of the same.

Merits:

- Third Party Outsourcing helps to focus more on core business activity and leverage the strategic strengths.

- Outsourcing helps cost savings therefore the need for more capital is reduced and efficiency increases.

- It helps to access latest newer techniques for ensuring operating efficiency.

- The process of outsourcing results, in reduction of overall costs which gives a competitive edge over others in the market.

- The need for licences, place, money, labour and other inputs including raw materials will be to the control and disposal of the producer.

- The operational challenges like controlling the labour and staff is vested with the third party who manages them.

- All taxation and other regulatory issues needs to be handled and addressed by the third-party producer.

- Outsourcing agency may be changed quickly and easily if it is not meeting the requirements of the entrepreneur Brand Owner.

However we need to discuss on the demerits of third party outsourcing:

- The outsourcing agency may not have the required wherewithal to discharge the obligations.

- The agency must be financially self-sufficient to discharge its obligations.

- The service delivery may not meet the expectations of the entrepreneur.

- Shift from one agency to an outsourcing agency may lead to delay and issues on finances including IPR.

- Quality if not controlled, may always be a victim in third party outsourcing.

- In light of the above, a decision needs to be taken whether to go for third party outsourcing or not.

(c) Job Work Model:

Job work model refers to supply of raw materials and all other related inputs to a job worker who will transform the same into finished goods at the unit belonging to the job worker.

The job work will be done as per the requirements of the entrepreneur who may or may not be the IPR owner. The job worker discharges his work in producing the goods as per the directives issued. This job work model may be suitable to products which has lesser inputs and production does not have technological complication. The compensation of the job worker is only for transformation of the input raw materials into commercially saleable form. In job work model the brand owner must make his investment in the raw materials, other inputs and send the same to the job worker for job work. Therefore the material cost rests with the brand owner. The job worker on the other hand may have to invest in capital assets like plant and machinery, buildings and other infrastructure required for the production of the goods. This model may be suitable to leverage costs, nevertheless the quality of the end product may suffer. So a call needs to be taken accordingly by the entrepreneur. on this based on his requirements.

(d) Off Shore Outsourcing Model:

Outsourcing of Products using the offshore resources is another way of sourcing. Offshore Outsourcing Model is suitable for service industries, which is cost effective. However certain cultural, language and other overseas issues needs to be handled and tackled correctly to be successful. It may therefore be necessary to weigh the merits and demerits of outsourcing before adopting the relevant model.

(e) Import of Goods by further processing/labelling:

Sourcing of products by import of goods from overseas countries may be done if the same is permitted and cost effective. Here the goods are imported in bulk quantities and thereafter value add, may or may not be done by the importer, who repacks and sells them in smaller quantities. This may be suitable for products like cosmetics, chemicals , oil, agricultural produce etc.

(f) Outsourcing through process production:

A Product may be outsourced through many segregated stages and passed directly to the next stage, where value add takes place. Here outsourcing may be done from different entities for various stages in the product. Such a process is financially cost effective and profitable. Outsourcing of different processes with different sources helps the producer to guard the secrets in the manufacturing of a final product. This will be suitable for a new product which needs different processes to produce the final product.

It may therefore be necessary to weigh the merits and demerits of outsourcing before adopting the relevant model or it combination, depending on one's business requirement.

Thus before choosing the model of sourcing and/or manufacturing it may be necessary by an entrepreneur to fulfil all the requisites as discussed in various chapters of this book and then take an informed decision.

CHAPTER FOUR

IPR COMPLIANCES

Need for Proactive Steps

Intellectual Property Rights (IPRs)

This is a very important aspect of compliance which needs to be adhered to, before planning for manufacture to launch the product.

Patents:

The object of granting patent under patent law is to encourage new inventions by giving a monopoly for a period of time to an inventor. This is because the inventor would have put his time, money, efforts, energy and knowledge in his invention which needs to be suitably rewarded for the same. An invention could also be kept as a trade secret. Trade secrets does not require registration under the patent law. Therefore care needs to be taken that the proposed product should not infringe/violate upon the Trade Secret/Patent possessed by such person/patent holder. This is a very critical aspect that needs to be checked up before the launch of the product. If the instant product proposed to be launched violates any of the patent rights, the holder of such patent rights may move before the appropriate forum by initiating appropriate proceedings for Infringement of Patent and also may seek a prohibitory injunction from launching or marketing of the product. If this aspect is not taken care, the entrepreneur will be saddled with huge losses arising out of the cost in manufacturing, launching and withdrawal of the product. In addition the product launch expenses, penalties and other financial costs also needs to be borne by him. To overcome this, a patent search needs to be done before the Patents Registry through a qualified accredited patent agent. There is a search facility available in the European Patent Organization (EPO) and United States Patent Organization (USPTO) where one can check for themselves whether the proposed product/ invention infringes any of the patent granted by the registry or patent application pending with the registry. These two registries can be termed as bench marks for any patent search registrations across the world. As a matter of abundant caution patent search may also be effected in the geography, where the proposed product is intended to be launched.

Thus through a diligent search it must be ensured that the proposed new product does not infringe upon the patent already granted. It is also necessary for an entrepreneur to know that there are two systems in the grant of patent, viz. Process Patent and Product Patent. Process Patent is the right granted by the Patent Authority of a country for *'manufacturing process'* and *not* for the *product per-se*. While in case of a Product Patent, it is an exclusive monopoly right given to the original inventor of a product. Product Patent is thus wide and gives absolute monopoly over the product. This means this right so given cannot be infringed through any processes. While in a Process Patent, a manufacturer cannot produce a Product by the "Patented Process", however there is no prohibition on him to produce the end product by employing another process not covered in the patent granted. Thus for an inventive product it is always better to file a patent application and seek protection under the Patent Laws. The patent is normally granted for a period of 20 years. In case of essential products like that of drugs/medicine/food articles the patent law normally provides for a lesser validity period say 10 years or so, which may vary from country to country. Infringing the patent of others will be very costly in terms of money, time, energy, penalty, damages and may bring an adverse publicity as a "*copy cat*". So utmost attention needs to be given to this aspect even before embarking upon manufacturing to launch the product.

Infringement of Patent:

Violation of the patent rights granted to a patent holder under the patent law constitutes infringement of patent. Intention to violate is not required for constituting an infringement under patent laws. The onus of establishing infringement is rested upon with the patent holder. If an entrepreneur has a doubt that his new product is likely to violate a patent in that case, he may out of an abundant caution approach the appropriate legal forum seeking declaration that any "*process or making*" which he is likely to produce does not constitute infringement. This may be resorted to if the law in that geography provides for such mechanism. If this is not possible then a written opinion need to be obtained from renowned scientists including attorneys, that the proposed product will not be violating the existing patent already granted to someone.

Action for Infringement of Patent:

Proceedings for infringement of patent must be filed in an appropriate forum against the alleged infringer. The proceedings for infringement of patent can be initiated only for the patent sealed/granted and not for the invention for which patent application made and pending for grant of patent.

Defences available in a Proceeding alleging Infringement of Patent:

- **The Plaintiff does not have the right to sue the alleged infringer:** If the plaintiff does not possess right from the original owner then he cannot initiate proceedings.

- **Alleged infringement is not inventive and obvious:** If the alleged infringement does not have inventive value and obvious, then infringement proceedings against the alleged infringer is not possible.

- **Revocation of patent by a legal forum:** If the registered patent is revoked by a competent legal forum including court, then infringement proceedings based on the subject patent is not possible.

- **Patent is within public domain:** If the subject patent is in the public domain, then there is no infringement necessitating proceedings.

- **Patent obtained by fraud:** If the patent is obtained by fraud, will be a valid defence in an infringement proceedings.

- **Invalid patent:** Infringement proceedings will not be possible for an alleged patent which has become invalid.

- **Laches – non initiation of timely action:** If the patent holder knowingly or otherwise, does not take timely action on the alleged infringer, then such in-action of the patent holder itself may be a valid defence in infringement proceedings.

- **Acquiescence:** When a patent holder indirectly permits other to use his patent, then he acquiesces himself, which could be a valid defence in the infringement proceedings.

- **Patent used for research/educational use:** If the patent is used for the furtherance of education and research without commercial significance could be a valid ground for defence in an infringement proceedings.

- **Permission to use the invention**: If permission is granted for the usage of the patented invention, then the holder of the patent cannot initiate proceedings for infringement against such bonafide user. Thus permission for use could be a valid defence in an infringement proceedings.

Reliefs available to a patent holder:

- **Interlocutory injunction:**

This is refers to interim/provisional prohibitory order issued by a legal forum against the infringer, who needs to stop the production forth with.

- **Award of damages:**

The legal forum may award damages as it may deem fit depending upon the loss that has been suffered by the patent holder due to the acts of the infringer.

- **Award of Penalties/Costs:**

The legal forums may award penalties/costs in addition to other reliefs.

- **Share in the Profits by seeking accounts:**

Depending on the claim, sometimes legal forums may seek accounts from the infringer and may order to share the profit for the wrongful enrichment made out of the patent.

- **Contempt Proceedings on violation of interim orders granted by legal forum/courts:**

On interim relief granted to an applicant if the other side does not comply the same, the applicant may initiate contempt of court proceedings and make the other party liable for penalties which may include imprisonment.

- **Order for destruction of impugned products:**

The courts/legal forums may order relief for destruction of impugned infringing products.

- **Appointment of Commissioner to visit the premises of the infringer and submit the required report:**

The courts/legal forums may direct the appointment of commissioner or competent officer to visit the premises of the infringer, take inventory of the stocks, records, other impugned materials and seek report to decide the infringement proceedings initiated by a patent holder. Therefore care needs to be taken to see that there is no patent infringement.

Trade Marks:

Similar to patents the next important aspect to be adhered and ensured is not to infringe upon the Trade Marks of others. Trade Mark refers to name, signature, mark, symbol, device or any one or more of its combination that recalls and distinguishes the products/services from that of another. Usage of a Trade Mark gives the user the rights to use and also register the same with the registry. A Trade Mark/Trade Name should not infringe upon another mark or even closely resemble such marks prevalent in the market. It is always good to ensure that the proposed Trade Mark is unique and a coined one. A common dictionary word for a Trade Mark cannot be a better idea to qualify as a trade mark.

The following, "Ten commandments of a Trade Mark" needs to be scrupulously followed, while adopting a Trade Mark of a product.

- Coined/Distinctive words are always a better bet in the selection of an ideal Trade Mark. The common general dictionary word which is not in use, will not give any monopoly over the usage. A coined un-used word will be a better bet for use as a trade mark.

- A Trade Mark which comprises of Common/Non-distinctive/Dictionary or any Laudatory Epithet, may not give monopoly over the Mark and its usage may invite costly litigation. This is because these common marks may be used by prior adopters and there may be bout of litigation to determine who the first prior user is.

- It is always necessary to make a National/International market search/Survey, to overrule the existence of the proposed trade mark. As discussed the trade mark should be unique and there should not be prior users of the same. So a detailed search needs to done to overrule its non-existence which helps in adopting the same as a new mark.

- Though trade mark, gives territorial monopoly, it always important not to use an identical/deceptive/similar/ well known/sounding marks as in existence anywhere. Usage of such marks must be avoided and the same could invite disputes followed by protracted litigations in legal forums. This will cause loss of time, money, business, penalties and damages.

- It is always necessary that a legal trade mark search is conducted in the Trade Mark Registry, in the respective identical classes of the proposed Trade Mark, to overrule its existence. A search can be effected by a Trade Mark Agent/Attorneys to overrule its existence and a formal written report may be obtained. A formal official search in the Trade Mark registry also helps in the adoption of a Trade Mark.

- Registration of trade mark under trademarks law, gives a prima-facie record of its ownership. Registration of a trade mark is not mandatory for its usage. However a registered trade mark helps in initiating infringement proceedings against an infringer. While, this may not be possible for an unregistered trade mark for which passing-off proceedings needs to be initiated under common law for its violation.

- The strength of the trade mark lies only on its usage, non-usage over a period may make the same invalid, notwithstanding its valid registration. Therefore a trade mark must be put into use to ensure its validity. Non usage of a mark for three years or so, takes away the monopoly over the usage of such mark.

- Thus when a mark is available for use, it is necessary to put the same into use to ensure monopoly and also register the same with trade mark registry for protection. It may also be necessary that the registered mark has to be renewed without fail by paying the required renewal fees to keep the same alive.

- To prove the usage of the trade mark it is essential to maintain an archive, with respect to its sales figures, advertisement/publicity expenses, press clippings, copies of hoardings, advertisement, and recordings of radio/television advertisement, tax assessments and vouchers/bills of the trade mark. This will help to establish the usage of the trademark to claim monopoly in a dispute and use the same in legal proceedings if need be.

- There should be no hesitation in seeking professional help wherever required or else the mistake may be sometimes very costly.

Method of Selecting a Trade Mark:

- Inputs from employees
- Using Consulting and Professional Advertising organizations
- Inputs from Sales, Product and Marketing Departments.
- Trade Mark Agents
- IPR Lawyers and Attorneys

Whatever may be the method used for selecting a Trade Mark, it is to be ensured that they are not common dictionary words and the mark is not used elsewhere. If a common weak mark is selected then it may be difficult to protect the same from users, who may try to ride on the reputation and equity already created over such mark. Therefore it is necessary to do a diligent search before the Trade Marks Registry backed up by an Internet Search to overrule the prior existence of the proposed Trade Mark. Thus as a matter of abundant caution it is always better to hire the services of a professional trade mark search firm of a standing to do a formal search and report existence of any such proposed mark. A written search report is usually given indicating identical marks and marks which have the similar pronunciation. Adopting a Trade Mark for a product without conducting availability search is very risky. If the subject Trade Mark infringes the other, infringement proceedings may be initiated by the Trade Mark Owner which may lead to prohibitory orders in the form of interim injunction followed by orders in the suit of infringement. Thus selecting the Trade Mark by an entrepreneur is an important business decision fraught with great commercial ramifications. The liability for infringement is usually determined by legal forums, if the Trade Marks are confusingly similar. Thus a formal Trade Marks search will help to avoid infringement claims arising out of its usage.

After overruling the existence of such Trade Mark, it would be always be in the interest of the entrepreneur to make a formal application before the Trade Mark Registry to make an application as a proposed user. Once the required formalities are completed in the Trade Mark Registry the Mark proceeds for registration. On registration the Trade Mark Owner is entitled to use the symbol ® to the right side, just above the mark so registered. The registration gives the ownership of the mark so registered and the registration certificate is prima-facie evidence to the ownership title of the trade mark in that geography.

The following factors are usually considered by legal forums in determining whether a Trade Mark infringes upon another registered Trade Mark:

- Trade Marks which are *identical* and the goods/services in which it is used is also *similar.*
- Trade Marks which are *similar* and goods/services in which it is used is also *similar.*
- Trade Marks which are *identical* and goods/services in which it is used are also *identical.*
- Stronger marks are given better protection than common weak marks.
- The intention of the person using the infringed mark is dishonest and want to derive benefit out of the good will/reputation of the registered trade mark.
- The Trade Mark creates confusion in the mind of the consumers.
- If both the original and infringing product are sold in the same retail shelf/counter.
- Using the marks after the expiry of the period of licence granted.
- Usage of registered trade mark on business papers/advertising without authorisation.
- Misrepresenting a product by trying to build a nexus with another Trade Mark without authorisation.

Thus while creating and adopting a Trade Mark the above factors needs to be kept in mind so that there is no scope for infringement.

Internet and Trade Marks:

The popularity of e-Commerce had given rise to host of issues in Trade Mark law. Trade Marks are infringed by people by creation of identical domain names. These people by blocking the names try to cash on the good will and reputation attached to such trade mark.

They are known as cyber squatters. Various legal forums across the globe give relief to the Trade Mark owners by recognising their IP rights. The domain dispute resolution mechanism of the WIPO also adjudicates and gives relief to the Trade Mark owners.

The following precautions needs to be adhered while using a Trade Mark:

- The launcher of a new product should not use the Trade Mark of the other in their Website or Web advertisements.
- The jurisdiction of a Trade Mark dispute in ecommerce could be a place where the website is accessible.
- Linking to another website cannot be resorted to without written permission.
- A deceptively similar Trade Mark of another should not be used.

- In addition to the Trade Mark even the Trade Names of another should not be used without the permission of the owner. Trade Name refers to the name and style under which a business/company operates upon, viz., **Vinayak** Financial Private Limited, **SMVBR** Realtors Limited, **Audi-Sundara** Real Estates LLP. Other than these trade name owners, these trade names cannot be used **as** *Trade/Service Marks* by other third parties in their respective fields viz. Finance, Realtors and Real Estates.

Thus if due care is taken on the above aspects, the launch of product will not subject to any legal hassles.

Rights of the Trade Mark owner against infringement/passing off:

Infringement refers to unauthorised use of a Registered Trade Mark, while proceedings against unauthorised usage of an unregistered Trade Mark can be initiated under the heading Passing-Off. The rights of a trade mark owner includes:

- Initiating proceedings for infringement under Trade Marks law.
- Relief may be sought for interlocutory injunction
- Claim for loss of profits and other penalties
- Contempt of court proceedings for non-compliance of interlocutory injunction/relief granted

- Seek revocation of the Trade Mark if the same is not valid.

The various Trade Mark Cases including the famous decided cases viz. (a) Louis Vuitton Vs. Louis Vuiton Dak (b) 3M Vs. 3N (c) Elvis Presley Vs. Brew Dog (d) Roche Products Limited Vs. Kent Pharmaceuticals Limited (e) Apple Corporation Vs. Apple Computer drives home the point that infringement of other's trade mark will be so costly to the infringer.

To protect from the same, today there are many agencies, which offers *"intelligent trademark search software"*. This Software has a built-in intelligence, which enables entrepreneurs to make a quick qualitative search to assess the possible risks in the adoption of proposed trade mark. This may be used effectively.

Copy Right:

Copyright is another specie of Intellectual Property Rights, which has assumed a prime place due to rapid advancement in the field of literature, art, artistic work, entertainment, music and software etc. Copyright is the right bestowed by the law to copy or reproduce a work in which copyright subsists. Thus the objective of copyright law is to encourage and reward authors, composers, artists including technocrats for their original works created by them, with a view to exploit the same for monetary gains. Like the Patent and Trade Marks, the label and the packing materials which has an artistic work over it, should not infringe upon other's product materials prevalent in the market. So necessary care needs to be taken to ensure that the proposed mark does not violate upon the copy right on such materials. Copy Right registration gives some added advantages over the Trade Mark Registration, so registration under Copy Right is also helpful for business.

Works in which Copyrights subsists from product stand point, includes variety of reference works, directories, advertising material, information compilation, computer programmes, catalogues, labels, artistic work and so on. So care should be taken to ensure there is no copy right violation on the packages/labels used over the product. It needs to be understood that copy right protection is not given to ideas, methods, systems, factual details, works that are in public domain, works of the government and so on.

What is copy right infringement?

It refers to unauthorized commercial exploitation of the copy right work of the copy right owner, without a license. The infringement may take the form of unauthorized usage of one's photograph, design, logos, text, videos and even an illustration used by one. The decision given in various copy right cases like Apple Vs. Google, Cariou Vs. Prince and Rogers Vs. Koons impresses upon the need, not to infringe upon the copy right of others which may be costly in terms of time, money, energy and damages.

What does not constitute infringement of Copy right:

- Fair dealing of literary, musical or artistic work will not constitute infringement.
- Reproduction by libraries for archival purposes
- If the copy right granted is not original as proved later
- Making few copies for having in the public library.
- Within public domain

Relief for copy right infringement:

- Cease and Desist notice followed by proceedings for infringement
- Relief of injunction
- Criminal Proceedings
- Seizure of impugned goods
- Award of damages and share in profits of the infringer.
- Costs

Therefore it needs to be ensured that the labels, packages, artistic work and other connected materials of the product does not infringe upon the copy right of another.

Confidential Information/Trade Secret:

Any information to qualify as a Confidential Information/Trade Secret, must be a secret, having commercial value, known only to limited people and diligently guarded. Coca-Cola beverage formulation is a best example for a trade secret which is meticulously protected since 1886 in USA.

Trade Secrets includes technical as well as commercial information or combination thereof which gives one competitive advantage.

While a product is launched it is also necessary that the confidential information/trade secret of the other is not used unauthorizedly either directly or indirectly in the launching of the product. Such trade secret information could be a formulation, process, method of manufacture etc. It is diligent and important not to employ personnel who were closely associated in the making of the product of a competitor or such similar goods. This is because the entrepreneur may be accused of using confidential information of the competitor and may seek cease and desist action in an appropriate legal forum. For example an IPR, being a secret formulation of a medicine is a trade secret, need not be registered under the patents act, such secret may be kept in private domain. This helps to enjoy the monopoly of such secret as a trade secret for several years endlessly, while registered patent for such formulation if granted will be in the public domain after say twenty years or after the expiry of the patent, allowing all to use the same freely.

An owner of a trade secret cannot restrain others from using the trade secret, if they have discovered the same on their own skill/efforts through reverse engineering process or through their own independent study. Thus trade secrets per-se do not grant monopoly legally as that of a patent.

If a trade secret is used unauthorizedly through espionage process or through privy of an interested person connected with the owner, then the owner of such trade secret may initiate legal proceedings against such user. The owner may also seek relief for return of confidential information, injunction against usage and seek damages for the unjust enrichment made. So great care needs to be taken not to use the trade secret/confidential information of the other.

Designs:

Another important aspect of the product launch which needs to be complied, is not to infringe upon the design rights of another. Registration of design under the relevant law helps to protect new or original designs. Design refers to the shape, configuration, pattern, with composition of colors, separate or combined, over the finished product which is judged solely by the eye. Purchase of a product from a consumer stand point is influenced not only by the usage efficiency, but also by the outer appearance of the product. So the package design should be original and must not violate the existing design. So care needs to be taken to verify the proposed design through design and net search. If the proposed design is unique and original then steps needs to be taken to register the same before commercial application. If the proposed design is in the public domain the same can be used freely. Un-authorized use of one's registered design is infringement and is liable for action. The registered design owner may seek relief against its usage by an unauthorized user and may seek compensation/damages in the infringement proceedings. Therefore care needs to be taken that the new product design/package does not infringe the registered design of another. Every country has a different set of laws governing the registration and enforcement of designs. In USA designs are registered under patent law. By filing one single international design patent application a design can be registered internationally. Only few limited countries facilitate international design patent registration through a single design patent application.

Design Infringement remedies:

The owner of a registered design on infringement of his design has the right to initiate civil proceedings in a court of law, seek interim relief in the form of prohibitory injunction order against usage, seek reimbursement for unjust enrichment and may claim damages for the same. So it is necessary to ensure that one's design should not infringe on the other.

Trade Dress:

Trade Dress is a development of recent years which refers to the visual appearance of a product clothed by a packaging that distinctly distinguishes itself from others. Many Countries in the world do not have a registration process for the same, but nevertheless this concept of trade dress is recognized across legal forums in the world. However in countries like USA registration of trade dress is provided for, which is valid for a period of ten years. The owner of a trade dress on infringement by an unauthorized user, has the right to initiate civil proceedings in a court of law, seek injunction against its usage and may claim damages for the same. Like other Intellectual Property Rights, sufficient care needs to be taken in not to infringing the Trade Dress of others.

CHAPTER FIVE

OTHER CRITICAL FACTORS IN PRODUCT LAUNCH:

Test Marketing
Product Claims
Legal Metrology Compliance
Storing Related Compliance
Usage Instructions
Consumer Activism

Test Marketing:

After developing the product, in order to know the pulse of the people including possible reactions of the public at large it is always better to Test Market the Product in a Geographical Territory. This helps to get a first-hand information on the usage, product delivery and satisfaction levels. Test Marketing is usually done to elicit the consumer behavior on the following:

- **Product trial**: It helps to know the mind-set of the consumer as to whether they will try the product so offered.

- **Frequency of purchase**: Test marketing helps to understand how frequently the consumer will purchase the product.

- **Repurchase**: It also helps to know whether the consumer will purchase the product again and again after the product trial.
- **Acceptance of the product**: Test marketing will give signals as to whether the accepted product by the consumer, will be subject to repeat purchases.

For ascertaining the above factors the test marketer may conduct the following tests:

1. Testing in selected geographic areas:

Under this, certain representative cities/towns are selected where the complete launching of the product is done from an aggressive sales promotion campaign to that of final sale. If the launch process is really successful in these representative places, this launch will be replicated in the whole geography of a country.

2. Sales Wave Research:

Under this process, samples of the product is offered to the consumer repeatedly free of cost. This process help to find the motivated mind set of the consumers to use the product when offered to them free of cost.

3. Shelf Test Marketing:

Under shelf test marketing, various sales outlets are selected in different geographies and the new product is displayed in the required shelves of a retail counter. These sales outlets are offered compensation for such display and sale. The testing entrepreneur will have the control over the said shelf. The publicity materials, freebies, pricing and offers will also be controlled by him. The consumer mindset is observed and based on the same the product is promoted in other areas.

4. Simulated Test Marketing:

Under simulated test marketing, batches of consumers are selected and invited to the sales outlet where they are allowed to buy goods at their preference. The new product is placed along with other competitor's product in the shelf, while the preference of the consumer is observed by their picking of their product choice. If the new product is not picked by them, free samples are distributed to them and their product experience feedback is collected personally or through telephone after few days.

Feedback thus obtained from the consumers is tabulated. The same is passed on to Research & Development, Packaging, Sales and Marketing for its immediate redressal wherever possible. This goes a long way in improving the final product basis the feedback thereby enhancing wider acceptability of the product.

Product Claims:

The claims that are made on the product delivery on usage of the product must be **real and true**. Therefore it would be prudent and in the interest of the entrepreneur to give attention and comply with the following:

1. Clinical Trials:

This refers to putting the instant product to trials in a clinical condition, observe the results and record the same. Based on the outcome of the results, the efficiency/efficacy of the product delivery needs to be documented. Such results may be used in a dispute to prove the efficacy of the product.

2. Opinion from Leading Scientists:

A written opinion may be obtained from few leading Scientists attached with reputed institutions of excellence, to substantiate the claims made on the product. The opinion needs to backed by factual information, data, scientific details and other references to substantiate the claims made on the product.

3. Consumer Survey:

A scientific and a proper survey may be conducted by delivering samples upfront to the consumers and their feedback duly documented. These records need to be preserved and kept in the archives of the organization and be used in appropriate forums to uphold the claims.

4. Collection of Scientific Literature:

Further to strengthen and substantiate the claims it may also be necessary to create an archive of scientific literature on the efficacy of the inputs used together with articles published in journals, magazines, books and other conferences.

5. Record of the Formulation Processes:

The processes of manufacture should be clearly documented batch wise on various inputs used and the process involved. These records must be carefully preserved in the archives and guarded till the product expiry period. This will help to prove that only established, good manufacturing practices were followed in the making of the final product.

6. Constant and Continuous Improvement:

On line with the changing manufacturing practices and usage of better inputs the product efficiency should undergo a change. This will send messages to the consumer that the organization delivers better products through continuous improvement and repose faith on delivering qualitative stuff. This culture if built even in the nascent stage of a product launch will draw more and more consumers confidently.

7. Statutory Specifications required for the product:

It is also necessary that the manufacturing and the end product confirms to the Statutory Specifications. For example in India we have the viz. Bureau of Indian Standards (BIS), Indian Standards Institution (ISI), Hazard Analysis Critical Control Point (HACCP), Food Safety Modernization Act (FSMA) etc. The product/services certification from International Organization for Standardization (ISO) will also add value to the end product. This will bring immediate acceptance on the products from the consumers by adding more reliability in meeting the anticipations of them. Entrepreneurs who source their products from third party producers may mandate them to get a relevant ISO Certification as a precondition to demonstrate that applicable standards were met in production. Every product and industry will have its own specifications which needs to be complied with.

8. Prohibition in the usage of certain ingredients:

The rules and regulations governing the production of the products may mandate or restrict usage of certain input/ingredients and other manufacturing practices in producing the product. Such stipulations needs to be scrupulously adhered to in the production of the product.

9. Endorsement as to its efficacy and towards favourable publicity:

A product in spite of its quality delivery, needs to be endorsed by celebrities, experts and even the common man after its use. These endorsers could really be brand ambassadors to enhance the confidence and increase the acceptability among more and more consumers. This helps to increase the sales volumes greatly.

10. Approvals/Licensing:

All approvals and licensing for the production of the product should be in place. Any amendments to the rules regulations emanating out of such approvals/licensing needs to be adhered then and there. This compliance will always be good in handling the regulatory authorities on compliance.

11. Conformity to Statutory Legal enactments:

Each and every product category may have numerous statutory enactments and other requirements which needs to be complied and the conditions fulfilled by an entrepreneur. Various products have different enactments like the Drugs and Cosmetics Act, Prevention of Food Adulteration Act, Pharmacy Act, Information Technology Act, Explosives Act, Mines Act, Electricity Act and so on. In addition to various sector specific enactments, It may be necessary to conform to the legislations like the Sale of Goods Act wherein the Conditions, Warranties and other stipulations contained therein including quality, fitness, merchantability and others needs to be fulfilled.

12. Permission for setting-up of the manufacturing unit of the products:

For Manufacturing it may be necessary to obtain permission from the Local Authority, State Authority and all other Statutory Authorities for Registration, Licensing, Starting, Producing, Storing and Selling the Products. A host of various enactments also needs to be followed and adhered to. A detailed Check List, containing the various Laws, Rules and Regulations needs to be made and compliance effected. This will give an utmost satisfaction of being a respectable law abiding due diligent corporate citizen.

Legal Metrology Compliance:

Legal Metrology refers to the Act, Rules, and Regulations which needs to be followed for products which are sold as packaged commodities. Product/Commodities which are not packed does not come under legal metrology law as the weighing of commodities are done before the consumer and the process of sale is instant. Further due to direct personal interaction by the buyer with the seller, the identity and other aspects of the product is known to the consumer. While in case of packaged goods, the producer's identity is not within the reach of the consumer. In view of this gap, legal metrology law mandates that the consumer should be provided with the required information such as the name and address of the producer, weight, MRP, name of the product, date of production, expiry date, batch no., license no., quantity, ingredients, customer service contact details for grievances and other declaration as may be necessary.

The Legal Metrology enactment aims to regulate the trade/commerce in weights, measures or numbers in the sale of packaged commodities through establishment/enforcement of standards of weights and measures. All packaged commodities should necessarily conform to these rules and non-adherence of the same may lead to initiation of proceedings by the legal metrological authorities before legal forums. Legal Metrology law may contain provisions for conviction of persons who were in-charge of such violations for second or subsequent offences committed. Therefore care needs to be taken to comply with the same.

Legal Metrology Law in most countries usually mandates the following requirements:

1. Legal Metrology Registration Certificate ought to be obtained by the manufacturer/packer/importer under the relevant rules.

2. Weights and Measures used in an establishment for dispensing the product should be verified and stamped by the legal metrology authority.

3. The above Certificate of Verification needs to be exhibited in the premises.

4. The mandatory declarations should be made over the pre-packaged products kept for sale.

5. The packaged goods should not be sold at a higher price than the price mentioned in the packages.

6. Test weight /measures need to be made available at selling point to ensure proper check of accuracy of a weighing instrument.

7. Renewal of licence for manufacturing of weights and measures needs to be done by the producer when the same is due.

8. In supermarkets, the electronic weighing machine with printer need to be kept for use by the consumers.

9. Renewal of licence for repair or sale of weights and measures together with records ought to be maintained by the manufacturer or repairer or dealer of weights and measures.

10. The seal affixed over the measures by the authority should be original.

Further, an owner of a Trade Mark is entitled to use the Mark ® over the Trade Mark to inform the outside world, signifying the mark has been registered. This has been provided for under the Trade Marks Act and may be mentioned in the package as well.

It also been a practice to use the word ™ near the Trade Mark to signify that the Registration of the said Trade Mark has been proposed and the Registration Application has been filed with the Trade Marks Registry over package. Likewise if the labels and packages are copyrighted, copy right claim may be made by indicating the mark, © over such label/package.

Storage related compliance of the product:

When the product is conceived and ready for marketing it is necessary to check out the statutory provisions governing the same for storage. If the product has to be sold by the reseller/stockist/distributor the law/rules and regulations as applicable to the product may mandate to obtain necessary license/approval from local authorities for storage of the same. So accordingly, this needs to be kept in mind and the cost of the same needs to be factored in the cost sheet. This portion of cost need to be reimbursed to the trade which needs to be incurred as out of pocket expenses. If license/approval is not obtained, the concerned statutory legislation may mandate seizure/imposition of penalty for the storage, whose action may stand in the way of free distribution and sale of the product. In certain geographies, oil products, crackers, fireworks, milk, fish, legal metrology weighing instruments and various such products, requires licence to store and sell the same. Therefore the requirements needs to be complied with before the launch.

Usage instructions of the product:

The usage of the product by the consumer needs to be educated especially when the product is new and unique requiring help in using them. Sometimes if the product is not used properly, by not adhering to the processes or the safeguards, the producer of the product may be made liable for the ill effects that may arise out of the product usage. Therefore it would be necessary to educate the consumer by providing a usage sheet/manual on how to use the product. This will help the ultimate consumer to use the product the way it is intended to be used to get the required results. The consumer should also be educated on the contra indications/effects that may likely to happen in using the product and steps needs to be taken for the same. This will help to mitigate the allergic ill effects that may arise in the usage of the product.

Consumer Activism - Need for some Proactive measures:

Today Consumer and Consumer Associations are very enlightened, active and conscious of their rights and approach consumer and other forums to espouse their rights against the producers. All producers are genuinely required to answer the gap arising out of "deficiency of service" over their products/services. There could be instances that products might not be stored properly, there could be instances of improper usage of product and so on which may not give the required results or cause harm. This outcome may rise to litigations which may be frivolous and sometimes even guided by mala-fide motives. It is necessary that the producer should be prepared to face the same. This requires qualified legal personnel should be taken on Board to oversee and handle such instances. These complaints needs to be handled judiciously without harming the interests of the producer. It should be the endeavour of the producer to address the genuine grievances of such complaints made. It may be necessary to test the product merchantability/suitability in accredited laboratories and supporting materials to that effect must be obtained. Samples of products in batches needs to be picked up, archived and preserved till the expiry of the product. This will help to meet out any such eventuality without much of strain/stress.

CHAPTER SIX

RISKS IN THE PRODUCT LAUNCH & AFTER

Risk Mitigation through Insurance

The end result of a product usage may bring some undesired results to the consumer, due to variety of factors viz. improper usage, inherent allergy, use of expired product, improper storage conditions of the product, bad inputs, spurious counterfeit products etc. Therefore care needs to be taken to protect from such claims/damages. Therefore it may be necessary to take some pro-active steps to counter the same. One such step is to take the required insurance covers to protect one self. This involves additional outflow and this cost should also be factored in determining the MRP of the product/ apportioned out of the projected profits.

The following insurance covers if taken may help mitigate the possible risks:

A. Commercial General Liability Insurance Policy

B. Errors and Omissions Liability Insurance Policy

C. Commercial Crime Liability Insurance Policy

D. Employers Liability Insurance Policy

E. Directors and Officers Liability Insurance Policy.

An indicative broad insurance coverage and its exclusions given by various insurance companies with respect to the above policies is detailed below:

A. Specimen Coverages in Commercial General Liability Insurance Policy:

The following are the indicative specimen coverage terms and conditions of a Commercial General Liability Insurance Policy. However the actual terms and conditions of a policy may vary based on circumstances prevailing at the relevant time. This insurance policy helps to mitigate risks arising out of Commercial General Liability.

Bodily Injury and Property Damage Liability

a. Under this policy, the insurer will pay those sums that the insured becomes legally obligated to pay as damages because of "bodily injury" or "property damage" and has the right to defend the insured against any "suit" seeking those damages. The insurer, at its discretion, may investigate any "occurrence" and settle any claim or "suit" that may result. The amount the insurer would pay for damages is limited to the limits specified in the policy.

b. This insurance applies to "bodily injury" and "property damage" only if:

i. The "bodily injury" or "property damage" is

caused by an "occurrence" that takes place in the "coverage territory";

ii. The "bodily injury" or "property damage" did not occur before the insurance commencement date, if any, shown in the declarations or after the end of the policy period; and

iii. A claim for damages because of the "bodily injury" or "property damage" is first made against any insured, in accordance with the policy conditions issued.

c. A claim by a person or organization seeking damages will be deemed to have been made when the notice of such claim is received or when the insurer effects settlement as stated above.

All claims for damages because of "bodily injury" to the same person, including damages claimed by any person or organization for care, loss of services, or death resulting at any time from the "bodily injury," will be deemed to have been made at the time the first of those claims is made against any insured. This applies to "property damage" as well.

The cover under this policy does not apply to the following exclusions:

a. Contractual Liability

"Bodily injury" or "property damage" for which the insured is obligated to pay damages by reason of the assumption of liability in a contract or agreement. This exclusion does not apply to liability for damages:

(i) That the insured would have in the absence of the contract or agreement; or

(ii) Assumed in a contract or agreement that is an "insured contract," provided the "bodily injury" or "property damage" occurs subsequent to the execution of the contract or agreement.

b. Workers' Compensation and similar Laws

Any obligation of the insured under a workers' compensation, disability benefits or unemployment compensation law or any similar law.

c. Employer's Liability

"Bodily injury" to:

(1) An "employee" of the insured arising out of and in the course of:

(a) Employment by the insured; or

(b) Performing duties related to the conduct of the insured's business; or

(2) The spouse, child, parent, brother or sister of that "employee"

This exclusion applies:

(1) When the insured is liable as an employer; and

(2) To any obligation to share damages with or repay someone else who must pay damages because of the injury.

This exclusion however does not apply to liability assumed by the insured under an "insurance contract."

d. Pollution

(1) "Bodily injury" or "property damage" arising out of the actual, alleged or threatened discharge, dispersal, seepage, migration, release or escape of pollutants:

(a) At or from any premises, site or location, which is or was at any time owned or occupied by, or rented or loaned to, any insured;

(b) At or from any premises, site or location which is or was at any time used by or for any insured or others for the handling, storage, disposal, processing or treatment of waste;

(c) Which are or were at any time transported, handled, stored, treated, disposed of, or processed as waste by or for any insured or any person or organization for whom the insured may be legally responsible; or

(d) At or from any premises, site or location on which any insured or any contractors or subcontractors working directly or indirectly on any insured's behalf are performing operations:

(i) If the pollutants are brought on or to the premises, site or location in connection with such operations by such insured, contractor or subcontractor; or

(ii) If the operations are to test for, monitor, clean up, remove, contain, treat, detoxify or neutralize, or in any way respond to, or assess the effects of pollutants.

(2) Any loss, cost or expense arising out of any:

(a) Request, demand or order that any insured or others test for, monitor, clean up, remove, contain, treat, detoxify or neutralize, or in any way respond to, or assess the effects of pollutants; or

(b) Claim or suit by or on behalf of a governmental authority for damages because of testing for, monitoring, cleaning up, removing, containing, treating, detoxifying or neutralizing, or in any way responding to, or assessing the effects of pollutants.

e. Aircraft, Auto or Watercraft

"Bodily injury" or "property damage" arising out of the ownership, maintenance, use or entrustment to others of any aircraft, "auto" or watercraft owned or operated by or rented or loaned to any insured. Use includes operation and "loading or unloading."

This exclusion does not apply to:

(1) Parking an "auto" on, or on the ways next to, premises the insured own or rent, provided the "auto" is not owned by or rented or loaned to the insured or the insured;

(2) Liability assumed under any "insured contract" for the ownership, maintenance or use of aircraft or watercraft; or

(3) "Bodily injury" or "property damage" arising out of the operation of any of the equipment listed.

f. War

"Bodily injury" or "property damage" due to war, whether or not declared, or any act or condition incident to war. War includes civil war, insurrection, rebellion or revolution. This exclusion applies only to liability assumed under a contract or agreement.

g. Damage to Property

"Property damage" to:

(1) Property owned by the insured, rent or occupied;

(2) Premises sold, given away or abandoned, if the "property damage" arises out of any part of those premises of the insured;

(3) Property loaned to the insured;

(4) That particular part of real property on which the insured or any contractors or sub-con-tractors working directly or indirectly on the insured's behalf are performing operations, if the "property damage" arises out of those operations; or

(5) That particular part of any property that must be restored repaired or replaced because "the insured's work" was incorrectly performed on it. The exclusions if any will be stated in the policy.

h. Damage to the insured's product

"Property damage" to "the insured's product" arising out of it or any part of it.

i. Damage to the insured's work

"Property damage" to "the insured's work" arising out of it or any part of it and included in the "products-completed operations hazard."

This exclusion does not apply if the damaged work or the work out of which the damage arises was performed on the insured's behalf by a subcontractor.

j. Damage to Impaired Property or Property Not Physically Injured

"Property damage" to "impaired property" or property that has not been physically injured, arising out of:

(1) A defect, deficiency, inadequacy or dangerous condition in "the insured's product" or "the insured's work"; or

(2) A delay or failure by the insured or anyone acting on the insured's behalf to perform a contract or agreement in accordance with its terms.

This exclusion does not apply to the loss of use of other property arising out of sudden and accidental physical injury to "the insured's product" or "the insured's work" after it has been put to its intended use.

k. Recall of Products, Work or Impaired Property

Damages claimed for any loss, cost or expense incurred by the insured or others for the loss of use, withdrawal, recall, inspection, repair, replacement, adjustment, removal or disposal of:

i. "The insured's product";

ii. "The insured's work"; or

iii. "Impaired property";

if such product, work or property is withdrawn or recalled from the market or from use by any person or organization because of a known or suspected defect, deficiency, inadequacy or dangerous condition in it.

l. Nuclear subject:

This policy does not cover liability for claims arising out of, directly or indirectly caused by or contributed to by:

(i) Ionizing radiations or contamination by radioactivity from any nuclear fuel or from any nuclear waste from the combustion of nuclear fuel;

(ii) Radioactive, toxic, explosive or other hazardous properties of any explosive nuclear assembly or nuclear component thereof;

Personal and Advertising Injury Liability:

The Insurer Company will pay those sums that the insured becomes legally obligated to pay as damages because of "personal injury" or "advertising injury" to which this insurance applies. Insurer have the right and duty to defend the insured against any "suit" seeking those damages. Further the insurer, at its discretion, investigate any "occurrence" or offense and settle any claim or "suit" that may result. But the damages is limited as described in the limits specified in the policy.

b. This insurance applies to:

(1) "Personal injury" caused by an offense arising out of the insured's business, excluding advertising, publishing, broadcasting or telecasting done by or for the insured;

(2) "Advertising injury" caused by an offense committed in the course of advertising the insured's goods, products or services; but only if:

(i) The offense was committed in the "coverage territory";

(ii) The offense was not committed before the insurance commencement date, if any, shown in the declarations or after the end of the policy period; and

(iii) A claim for damages because of the "personal injury" or "advertising injury" is first made against the insured, subject to the terms and conditions contained therein.

Exclusions - This insurance does not apply to:

a. "Personal injury" or "advertising injury":

(i) Arising out of oral or written publication of material, if done by or at the direction of the insured with knowledge of its falsity;

(ii) Arising out of oral or written publication of material whose first publication took place before the Retroactive Date, if any, shown in the declarations;

(iii) Arising out of the wilful violation of a penal statute or ordinance committed by or with the consent of the insured;

For which the insured has assumed liability in a contract or agreement. This exclusion does not apply to liability for damages that the insured would have in the absence of the contract or agreement; or

(iv) Arising out of the actual, alleged or threatened discharge, dispersal, seepage, migration, release or escape of pollutants at any time.

b. "Advertising injury" arising out of:

(i) Breach of contract, other than misappropriation of advertising ideas under an implied contract;

(ii) The failure of goods, products or services to conform with advertised quality or performance;

(iii) The wrong description of the price of goods, products or services; or

c. Any loss, cost or expense arising out of any:

(i) Request, demand or order that any insured or others test for, monitor, clean up, remove, contain, treat, detoxify or neutralize, or in any way respond to, or assess the effects of pollutants; or

(ii) Claim or suit by or on behalf of a governmental authority for damages because of testing for, monitoring, cleaning up removing, containing, treating, detoxifying or neutralizing, or in any way responding to, or assessing the effects of pollutants.

Medical Payments:

a. The Insurer will pay medical expenses as described below for "bodily injury" caused by an accident:

(i) On premises the insured own or rent;

(ii) On ways next to premises the insured own or rent; or

(iii) Because of the insured's operations;

This is however subject to certain terms and conditions contained therein in the policy contract.

b. The Insurer will make these payments regardless of fault. These payments will not exceed the applicable limit of insurance. The insurer will pay reasonable expenses for:

(i) First aid administered at the time of an accident;

(ii) Necessary medical, surgical, x-ray and dental services, including prosthetic devices; and

(iii) Necessary ambulance, hospital, professional nursing and funeral services.

The Insurance Company will not pay expenses for "bodily injury" concerning the following exclusions:

a. To anyone other than the insured.

b. To a person hired to do work for or on behalf of any insured or a tenant of any insured.

c. To a person injured on that part of premises the insured own or rent that the person normally occupies.

d. To a person, whether or not an "employee" of any insured, if benefits for the "bodily injury" are payable or must be provided under a workers' compensation or disability benefits law or a similar law.

e. To a person injured while taking part in athletics including persons in hazardous operations.

f. Due to war, whether or not declared, or any act or condition incident to war. War includes civil war, insurrection, rebellion or revolution.

The Policy will also have provisions for supplementary payments for coverage listed above. If the insured is declared as a corporation or organization other than a partnership or joint venture, the insured and the insured subsidiaries, group companies are insured. This also includes, the insured employees, executive officers and directors of the insured, only for the conduct of the insured's business within the scope of their employment or their duties as executive officers or directors.

The limits of insurance, the commercial liability conditions, general liability conditions, general definitions, other supplementary terms and conditions including arbitration are also part of the policy document.

B. Specimen Coverages in Errors and Omissions Liability Policy:

The following are the specimen coverage and terms and conditions of an Errors and Omissions Liability Insurance Policy. The following terms and conditions are only illustrative and may vary based on circumstances and conditions prevailing at a relevant time.

Professional and Technology Based Services:

To pay on behalf of the the insured - Damages and Claims Expenses, in excess of the Deductible, which the Insured shall become legally obligated to pay because of any Claim first made against any Insured and reported to the Underwriters during the Period of Insurance or Extended Reporting Period arising out of any actual or alleged negligent act, error or omission, breach of duty, mis-statement, misrepresentation or any unintentional breach of contract in rendering or failure to render professional Services or technology based services on or after the retroactive date set forth in the declarations and before the end of the period Insurance by the Insured or by any person, including an independent contractor, for whose negligent act, error or omission or unintentional breach of contract the insured organization is legally responsible.

Technology Products:

To pay on behalf of the insured - damages and claims expenses, in excess of the deductible, which the insured shall become legally obligated to pay because of any claim first made against any insured and reported to the underwriters during the period of insurance of extended reporting period (if applicable) arising out of actual or alleged negligent act, error or omission, breach of duty, mis-statement, misrepresentation or any unintentional breach of contract by the Insured on or after the insurance commencement date set forth in the declarations and before the end of the period of insurance that results in the failure of technology products to perform the function or serve the purpose intended.

Computer Network Security:

To pay on behalf of the insured - damages and claims expenses, in excess of the deductible, which the insured shall become legally obligated to pay because of any claim first made against any insured and reported to underwriters during the period of insurance or extended reporting period (if applicable) arising out of actual or alleged negligent act, error or omission, breach of duty, mis-statement, misrepresentation or any unintentional breach of contract on or after the retroactive date in the declarations and before the end of the period of insurance in the course of providing or managing computer systems security by the insured or by any person, including an independent contractor, for whose act, error or omission the insured organization is legally responsible that results in:

1. The inability of a third party, who is authorized to do so, to gain access to computer systems or the insured technology based services;

2. The failure to prevent unauthorized access to computer systems that results in:

(a) the destruction, deletion, corruption or inclusion of any malicious code on electronic data on computer systems;

(b) theft of data from computer systems, or

(c) denial of service attacks against internet sites or computers; or

3. the failure to prevent transmission of malicious code from computer systems, to third party computers and systems.

Multimedia and Advertising:

To pay on behalf of the insured - damages and claims expenses, in excess of the deductible, which the insured shall become legally obligated to pay because of liability imposed by law or assumed under contract resulting from any claim first made against any insured and reported to underwriters during the period of insurance or extended reporting period (if applicable) arising out of one or more of the following acts committed on or after the retroactive date set forth in the declarations and before the end of the period of insurance in the course of the insured organization's performance of professional services, media activities or technology based services or provision of technology products;

(i) defamation, libel, slander, product disparagement, trade libel, prima facie tort, infliction of emotional distress, outrage, outrageous conduct, or any other tort(including personal injury claims) whether in the oral or written form, relating to disparagement or harm to the reputation or character of any person or organization.

(ii) invasion of or interference with the right to privacy or of publicity;

(iii) mis-appropriation of any name or likeness for commercial advantage;

(iv) false arrest, detention or imprisonment or malicious prosecution;

(v) invasion of or interference with any right to private occupancy, including trespass wrongful entry, eviction or eavesdropping;

(vi) plagiarism, piracy or misappropriation of ideas under implied contract;

(vii) actual or alleged infringement of copyright;

(viii) actual or alleged infringement of trade dress, domain name, title or slogan, or the dilution or infringement of trademark or service mark in any manner whatsoever;

(ix) negligence regarding the content of any Media Communication, including harm caused through any reliance or failure to rely upon such content;

(x) actual or alleged infringement of patents, misappropriation of trade secret or any other intellectual property right.

The coverage stated above shall not apply to any claim for or arising out of the disclosure, misuse or misappropriation of any ideas, trade secrets or confidential information that came into the possession of any person prior to the date he or she became an employee, officer, director, principal or partner of the insured organization.

Exclusions:

The coverage under this Insurance does not apply to damages or claims expenses in connection with or resulting from any Claim:

a. Arising out of or resulting from any criminal, dishonest, fraudulent or malicious act, error or omission committed by any Insured; however, this Policy shall apply to Claims Expenses incurred in defending any such Claim alleging the foregoing until such time as there is a final adjudication, judgment, binding arbitration decision or conviction against the Insured, or admission by the Insured, establishing such criminal, dishonest, fraudulent or malicious conduct, or a plea of nolo contendere or no contest regarding such conduct, at which time the Named Insured shall reimburse Underwriters for all Claims Expenses incurred defending the Claim and Underwriters shall have no further liability for Claims Expenses;

b. Arising out of or resulting from any act, error or omission committed prior to the inception date of this Insurance:

- if any Insured on or before the inception date knew or could have reasonably foreseen that such act, error or omission might be expected to be the basis of a Claim; or

- in respect of which any Insured has given notice of a circumstance which might lead to a Claim to the insurer of any other policy in force prior to the inception date of this Policy;

c. Arising out of any related or continuing acts, errors or omissions where the first such act, error or omission was committed prior to the Retroactive Date.

d. For, arising out of, or resulting from Bodily Injury or Property Damage;

e. Arising out of or resulting from any actual or alleged obligation to make licensing fee or royalty payments, including but not limited to the amount of timeliness of such payments;

1. For or arising out of or resulting from any costs or expenses incurred or to be incurred by the Insured or others for the reprinting, recall, removal or disposal of any Media Material, including any media or products containing such Media Material; or

2. the withdrawal, recall, inspection, repair, replacement, reproduction, removal or disposal of:

(a) Technology Products, including any products or other property of others that incorporate Technology Products;

(b) work product resulting from or incorporating the results of Professional Services or Technology Based Services; or

(c) any products or other property on which Professional Services or Technology Based Services are performed;

However this exclusion shall not apply to third party claims for the resulting loss of use of such media material or technology products, or loss of use of the work product resulting from such professional services or technology based services;

f. Arising out of or resulting from the failure of Computer Systems to be protected by security practices and procedures equal to or superior to those disclosed in response to questions in the Application for Insurance relating Computer Systems security, including access protection, intrusion detection, data back-up procedures, Malicious Code protection, and data encryption procedures; or

g. Arising out of, resulting from or alleging:

1. any failure or malfunction of electrical or telecommunications infrastructure or services, unless under the Insured Organization's operational control; or

2. fire, flood, earthquake, volcanic eruption, explosion, lighting, wind, hail, tidal wave, landslide, act of God or other physical event;

h. Made by any business enterprise in which any Insured has greater than a certain ownership interest or made by any parent company or other entity which owns more than certain percentage of the Named Insured, or arising out of or resulting from any Insured's activities as a trustee, partner, officer, director or employee of any employee trust, charitable organization, corporation, company or business other than that of the Insured Organization;

i. Arising out of Professional Services, Media Activities or Technology Based Services performed for any entity, or Technology Products provided to any entity

j. Arising out of or resulting from the insolvency or bankruptcy of any Insured or of any other entity including but not limited to the failure, inability, or unwillingness to pay Claims, losses, or benefits due to the insolvency, liquidation or bankruptcy of any such individual or entity;

k. For or arising out of or resulting from:

1. any employer - employee relations, policies, practices, acts or omissions, or any actual or alleged refusal to employ any person, or misconduct with respect to employees, whether such Claim is brought by an employee, former employee, applicant for employment, or relative of such person;

2. any actual or alleged discrimination of any kind including but not limited to age, color, race, sex, creed, national origin, marital status, sexual preference, disability or pregnancy;

3. any actual or alleged act, error or omission or breach of duty by any director or officer in the discharge of their duty if the Claim is brought by the Named Insured, a Subsidiary, or any directors, officers, stockholders, or employees of the Named Insured or a Subsidiary in his or her capacity as such;

4. Either in whole or in part, directly or indirectly, arising out of or resulting from or in consequence of, or in any way involving:

5. Asbestos, or any materials containing asbestos in whatever form or quantity;

6. The actual, potential, alleged or threatened formation, growth, presence, release or dispersal of any fungi, molds, spores or mycotoxins of any kind;

7. Underwriters will have no duty or obligation to defend any Insured with respect to any Claim or governmental or regulatory order, requirement, directive, mandate or decree which either in Whole or in part, directly or indirectly, arises out of or results from or in consequence of, or in any way involves the actual, potential, alleged or threatened formation, growth, presence, release or dispersal of any fungi, molds, spores or mycotoxins of any kind;

8. the existence, emission or discharge of any electromagnetic field, electromagnetic radiation or electromagnetism that actually or allegedly affects the health, safety or condition of any person or the environment, or that affects the value, marketability, condition or use of any property; or

9. the actual, alleged or threatened discharge, dispersal, release or escape of Pollutants; or any governmental, judicial or regulatory directive or request that the Insured or anyone acting under the direction or control of the Insured test for, monitor, clean up, remove, contain, treat, detoxify or neutralize Pollutants. Pollutant means any solid, liquid, gaseous or thermal irritant or contaminant including gas, acids, alkalis, chemicals, heat, smoke, vapor, soot, fumes or waste.

C. Specimen Coverages in Commercial Crime Insurance Policy:

The following are the specimen coverage and terms and conditions of a Commercial Crime Insurance Policy. The following terms and conditions are only illustrative in nature and may vary based on various circumstances and conditions prevailing at the relevant time.

What is covered?

1. Employee Theft:

Insurance Company will pay for loss of or damage to "money", "securities" and "other property" resulting from "theft" committed by an "employee", whether identified or not, acting alone or in collusion with other persons.

2. Forgery or alteration:

a. Insurance Company will pay for loss resulting from "forgery" or alteration of checks, drafts, promissory notes, or similar written promises, orders or directions to pay a sum certain in "money" that are:

(1) Made or drawn by or drawn upon the insured; or

(2) Made or drawn by one acting as the insured's agent; or that are purported to have been so made or drawn.

b. If the insured is sued for refusing to pay any instrument, on the basis that it has been forged or altered, the insured have the written consent to defend against the suit and Insurance Company will pay for any reasonable legal expenses that the insured may incur and pay in that defense. The amount that Insurance Company will pay is in addition to the Limit of Insurance applicable to this Insuring Agreement.

3. Inside the Premises -Theft of Money and Securities

a. Insurance Company will pay for loss of "money" and "securities" inside the "premises" or "banking premises" resulting from "theft", disappearance or destruction.

b. Insurance Company will pay for loss from damage to the "premises" or its exterior resulting directly from an actual or attempted "theft" of "money" and "securities", if the insured are the owner of the "premises" or are liable for damage to it.

c. Insurance Company will pay for loss of or damage to a locked safe, vault, cash register, cash box or cash drawer located inside the "premises" resulting directly from an actual or attempted "theft" of or unlawful entry into those containers.

4. Inside the Premises - Robbery or Safe Burglary of other Property

a. Insurance Company will pay for the loss of or damage to "other property":

(1) Inside the "premises" resulting from an actual or attempted "robbery" of a "custodian"; or

(2) Inside the "premises" in a safe or vault resulting directly from an actual or attempted "safe burglary".

b. Insurance Company will pay for loss from damage to the "premises" or its exterior resulting directly from an actual or attempted "robbery" or "safe burglary" of "other property", if the insured are the owner of the "premises" or are liable for damage to it.

c. Insurance Company will pay for loss of or damage to a locked safe or vault located inside the "premises" resulting from an actual or attempted "robbery" or "safe burglary".

5. Outside the premises

a. Insurance Company will pay for loss of "money" and "securities" outside the "premises" in the care and custody of a "messenger" or an armored motor vehicle company resulting from "theft", disappearance or destruction.

b. Insurance Company will pay for loss of or damage to "other property" outside the "premises" in the care and custody of a "messenger" or an armored motor vehicle company resulting directly from an actual or attempted "robbery".

6. Computer/Electronic and Electronic Funds Transfer fraud.

Insurance Company will pay for loss of or damage to "money", "securities" and "other property" resulting directly from the use of any computer or other electronic system or Electronic Funds Transfer to fraudulently cause a transfer of that property from inside the "premises" or "banking premises":

a. To a person (other than a "messenger") outside those "premises";or

b. To a place outside those "premises".

7. Money orders and counterfeit paper currency

Insurance Company will pay for loss resulting directly from the insured having accepted in good faith, in exchange for merchandise, "money" or services:

a. Money orders issued by any post office, express company or bank that are not paid upon presentation; or

b. "Counterfeit" paper currency that is acquired during the regular course of business.

8. Defence Costs

Insurance Company will pay for reasonable defense costs the insured may have to incur in defending any of the above covered acts. Defence costs do not carry any deductibles.

The limit of insurance will be for loss in any one "occurrence" is the applicable Limit of Insurance shown in the declarations. The Insurance Company will not pay for loss in any one "occurrence" unless the amount of loss exceeds the deductible amount shown in the declarations. In the event more than one deductible amount could apply to the same loss, only the highest deductible amount may be applied.

Exclusions - This Policy does not apply to:

a. Acts committed by the insured, the insured partners, the insured members or the insured employees - Loss resulting from any dishonest act committed by the insured, the insured partners or the insured employees whether acting alone or in collusion with other persons.

b. Acts of Employees, Managers, Directors, Trustees or Representatives - Loss resulting from any dishonest act committed by any of the insured "employees", "managers", directors, trustees or authorized representatives:

(i) Whether acting alone or in collusion with other persons; or

(ii) While performing services for the insured or otherwise; except when covered under the policy.

c. Governmental Action- any direct loss resulting from seizure or destruction of property by order of a Governmental Authority.

d. Indirect loss- any loss that is an indirect result of any act or "occurrence" covered by this policy including, but not limited to, loss resulting from:

(1) The insured's inability to realize income that the insured would have realized had there been no loss of or damage to "money" "securities" or "other property".

(2) Payment of damages of any type for which the insured is legally liable.

(3) Payment of costs, fees or other expenses the insured incur in establishing either the existence or the amount of loss under this policy.

e. Nuclear – any loss resulting from nuclear reaction, nuclear radiation or radioactive contamination, or any related act or incident.

f. War and similar actions – any loss resulting from war, whether or not declared, warlike action, insurrection, rebellion or revolution, or any related act or incident.

D. Specimen Coverages in Employer's Liability Policy:

The following are the specimen coverage and terms and conditions of an Employers Liability Insurance Policy. The following terms and conditions are only illustrative in nature and not exhaustive. Actual terms and conditions of a policy may vary based on various circumstances and conditions prevailing at the relevant time.

1. The insurer shall pay those losses arising out of the insured's wrongful employment act against the insured's employees, to which this insurance applies. The wrongful employment act must commence or take place after the original inception date, but before the end of the policy period. A claim or suit for a wrongful employment act must be first made against the insured during the policy period or any extended reporting period (if applicable) and reported to the insurer pursuant to the terms of this policy.

2. A claim or suit by a person or organization seeking damages will be deemed to have been made at the earlier of the following times:

a. When written notice of such claim or suit is received and recorded by any insured or by us, whichever comes first; or

b. When the insurer makes settlement in accordance with the terms of this Policy.

B. Defense:

1. The insurer has the right to defend and appoint an attorney to defend any claim or suit brought against any insured for a wrongful employment act to which this insurance applies, even if the claim or suit is groundless or fraudulent.

2. The insurer have the right to investigate and settle any claim or suit that it believes to be proper.

3. The insurer shall pay all reasonable costs the insured may incur while defending a claim or suit, subject to agreed limits.

4. The insurer shall pay premiums for appeal bonds, or bonds to release property being used to secure a legal obligation, for a covered suit subject to certain conditions.

5. The insurer shall pay the costs against an insured in a suit defended.

6. Payments for defence costs are included within the limit of liability.

7. The insurer shall pay all interest on that amount of any judgment within the limit of liability:

a. which accrues after entry of judgment; and

b. before the insurer pay, offer to pay, or deposit in court that part of the judgment within the applicable Limit of Liability.

Exclusions - This insurance does not apply to:

A. Profit or Advantage: Any liability arising out of the gaining of any profit or advantage to which an insured was not legally entitled. However, to the extent that a claim or suit is otherwise covered under the policy, the insurer will defend a claim or suit asserting that an insured gained a profit or advantage to which the insured was not legally entitled, until such time as the insured is determined to have gained a profit or advantage to which the insured was not legally entitled;

B. Criminal Acts: Any liability arising out of any dishonest, fraudulent, criminal, or malicious act by any insured. However, to the extent that a claim or suit is otherwise covered under the policy, the insurer will defend a claim or suit asserting a dishonest, fraudulent, criminal or malicious act until such time as the insured is determined to have committed such dishonest, fraudulent, criminal or malicious act;

C. Property Damage: Any liability arising out of property damage;

D. Bodily Injury: Any liability arising out of bodily injury;

E. Worker's Compensation, Social Security and Unemployment, Disability and Retirement

Any liability arising out of any obligation pursuant to any worker's compensation, disability benefits, unemployment compensation, unemployment insurance, retirement benefits, social security benefits or similar law.

This exclusion, however, shall not apply to loss arising from a claim or suit for retaliation;

F. Contractual Liability: Any liability arising out of any actual contractual liability of any insured under any express contract or agreement. This exclusion, however, shall not apply to the extent any liability does not arise under such express contract or agreement;

G. Non-Monetary Relief - including but not limited to:

(1) injunctive relief;

(2) declaratory relief;

(3) job reinstatement;

H. Prior Knowledge – of any liability arising out of incidents, circumstances or wrongful employment acts, which an insured, prior to the original inception date as shown in the Declarations, had knowledge of;

I. Prior Notice – of any liability arising out of the facts alleged, or to the same or related wrongful employment acts alleged or contained in any claim or suit which has been reported, or in any circumstances of which notice has been given, under any policy of which this policy is a renewal or replacement or which it may succeed in time;

J. Securities Holder - Any claim or suit brought by a securities holder of the insured in their capacity as such, whether directly, derivatively on behalf of the insured, or by class action;

Who is an insured?

If the insured are shown in the declarations as a corporation or organization other than a partnership or joint venture, the insured and the insured subsidiaries, group companies are insured. The insured employees, executive officers and directors are insured, only for the conduct of the insured's business within the scope of their employment or their duties as executive officers or directors.

Extensions of this policy:

1. Subject otherwise to the terms hereof, this policy shall cover loss arising from any claims or suits made against the estates, heirs, or legal representative of deceased individual insured, and the legal representatives of individual insured, in the event of incompetency, who were individual insured at the time the wrongful employment acts, upon which such claims or suits are based, were committed.

2. Subject otherwise to the terms hereof, this policy shall cover loss arising from all claims and suits made against the spouse (whether such status is derived by reason of statutory law, common law or otherwise of any applicable jurisdiction in the world) of an individual insured, including a claim or suit that seeks damages recoverable from marital community property, property jointly held by the individual insured and the spouse, or property transferred from the individual insured to

the spouse; provided, however, that this extension shall not afford coverage for a claim or suit arising out of any wrongful employment act of the spouse, but shall apply only to claims or suits arising out of any wrongful employment acts of an individual insured, subject to the policy's terms, conditions and exclusions.

Limit of liability:

A. The aggregate limit of liability shown in the declarations limits what the insurer will pay for all loss arising out of claims first made against insured during the policy period regardless of:

1. the number of persons or organizations covered by this policy; or

2. the number of claims made or suits brought; or

3. the length of the policy period.

B. The aggregate limit of liability is the most the insurer need to pay for all losses covered under this policy, including amount incurred for defense costs.

C. The aggregate limit of liability for the extended reporting period shall be part of, and not in addition to the aggregate limit of liability for the policy period.

D. Subject to the aggregate limit of liability, each wrongful employment act is the most one for which the insurer pays for loss.

E. All claims and suits arising from the same or related wrongful employment acts shall be treated as arising out of a single wrongful employment act.

F. All claims or suits arising out of one wrongful employment act shall be deemed to be made on the date that the first such claim is made or suit is brought. All claims asserted in a class action suit will be treated as arising out of a single wrongful employment act.

(E) Directors and Officers Liability Insurance Policy:

The Directors and Officers Liability Insurance policy covers liability arising out of the conduct and discharge of their respective duties, including costs to defend any civil and/or criminal action against the Directors and/or Officers. Such proceedings may be initiated against the Directors and/or Officers by Shareholders, Employees, Consumers, Competitors or Members of the General public, Banks, Financial Institutions or even Government authorities.

This policy however does not cover:
- Liability arising out of Criminal Acts
- Physical injury and Damage to Property
- Infringement of IPRs
- Penalties for commission of Torts
- Proceedings already pending in courts including class action suits.

Thus by taking the above covers the risks can be mitigated. It should be clear that exclusions cannot be claimed in the policy. Therefore it is necessary that an appropriate cover needs to be taken tailoring the needs of the producer who wants to launch his product. Initially a simple cover may be taken. Larger cover with better inclusions may be taken once the business improves. Various other insurance covers to mitigate risk includes, property all risk insurance, business interruption insurance, automobile liability insurance, workmen compensation insurance, EDP cybercrime insurance and so on. These covers may be taken based on necessity and business growth.

Compliant Organization:

In addition to the above as discussed the producer of goods should always aim for being a compliant organization. Compliance of Law, Rules, Regulations and other requirements to its letter and spirit will give enough strength and confidence in facing any situations.

As mentioned elsewhere in this book, there should proper back up on claims made on the product and its end use. All these backups should be preserved in the archives. These records will serve handy in handling disputes that may occur and for defending the same.

In addition every activity needs to be documented and due control exercised properly at all stages. This sort of responsible compliant organization will help to face any perceived inherent risks with confidence and defend the same successfully.

CHAPTER SEVEN

COMPLIANCE REQUIREMENTS

Comprehensive Check List, in each Geography

We have discussed various facets of compliance and preparedness in the launch of a product. Thus the book captures the indicative requirements in the launch of product with an **overall 360° view.**

The requirements and preparedness may change from one geography to geography. This may also vary from time to time. Therefore on the basis of the requirements mentioned herein an exhaustive comprehensive check list clearly mentioning the applicable Legislations/Rules/Regulations/Requirements and other specifics needs to be captured in total and suitably documented. Meticulous care should be taken to ensure that all the requirements are carefully captured. The compliance levels needs to be marked and non-compliance needs to be monitored closely and complied with. This will certainly help to smoothly launch the product. A detailed checklist will facilitate better control, and no violations if any should ever come as a surprise affecting the smooth launch of the product.

The Check List may primarily consist of the following aspects:

a. Regulatory aspects in manufacturing.

b. Compliance aspects in the launch of the product and required timelines.

c. Legislations, Rules and Regulations applicable to that product /services category and compliance thereof.

d. Budget for scheduled and unscheduled expenses.

e. Plan and Route Map for the product launch.

f. Incentives, Publicity Materials, Advertisement and below the line sales promotion strategies.

g. Agencies to promote customer relations.

h. Distribution of the products to all counters.

i. Well-oiled distribution channel to cater to the demand then and there.

j. Sales and Marketing co-ordination.

k. Constitution of Sales Task force

l. Cross functional committee consisting of Sales, Marketing, Legal, Research and Development, Logistics, Sourcing and other required department personnel.

m. Constant monitoring of the market.

n. Eye on the competition and devising strategies to overcome the same.

In addition to the above, there may be other factors which may differ from an organization to another, geography to geography, product to product, which needs to suitably captured, compliance effected, followed up and corrective steps taken then and there.

If this is done diligently, an entrepreneur can easily manage any issues that may confront him in the launch of product/services and make it really successful.

******

INDICATIVE TASK RESPONSIBILITY CHART IN PRODUCT LAUNCH

No.	Pre-requisites	Departments involved	Tasks	Owner		Completion Date	Status
				Primary	Secondary		
1.	Conceiving the Product	Promoters assisted by New Product Team	Clearance of Launch	Promoters	New Product Team	___Days, By date___	
2.	Cost Sheet	Costing/Finance/ New Product Team	Cost Evaluation	New Product Team	Costing/Finance		
3.	Fixation of MRP	New Product Team/Finance/ Marketing	Best Price	New Product Team	Marketing/Finance		
4.	Pricing Regulatory Compliance	Marketing/Finance/Legal	Compliance	Marketing / Finance	Legal		
5.	Sourcing Model	Sourcing/Finance/ New Product Team	Right Model	Sourcing	Finance/New Product Team		

6.	IPR Compliances					
	Patent & Designs	Research & Development/New Product Team/Legal	No Infringement	R&D	New Product Team/Legal	
	Trade Mark & Copy Right	New Product Team/Marketing/Legal	No Infringement	New Product Team	Marketing/Legal	
	Trade Secrets/Confidential Information	Research & Development/New Product Team/Human Relations/Legal	No Unauthorised Usage	R&D/New Product Team/Human Relations	Legal	
7.	Risks	New Product Team/R&D/Finance/Risk/Insurance	No/Lesser Risks - Mitigation	R&D/New Product Team	Finance/Risk/Insurance	
8.	Test Marketing	New Product Team/Marketing/R&D	Product Evaluation and Feedback	New Product Team/Marketing	R&D	
9.	Product Claims	R&D/New Product Team/Marketing/Legal	Bonafide Product Claims	R&D/New Product Team	Marketing/Legal	

10.	**Legal Metrology**		**Legal Metrology Compliance**		Marketing/Legal
11.	Storing	New Product Team/ Infrastructure/ Administration/Marketing	Storing Compliance	New Product Team/ Infrastructure/ Administration	Marketing
12.	Usage Instructions	New Product Team/ R&D/ Marketing	**Safe and Proper Usage**	New Product Team/ R&D	Marketing
13.	Consumers	New Product Team/ Marketing/R&D / Legal	**Product Satisfaction including handling**	New Product Team/ Marketing	R&D/Legal
14.	Detailed Checklist – In every Geography	New Product Team/ Country Manager -Marketing/R&D /Legal	Compliance	New Product Team/ Marketing	R&D/Legal

ABOUT THE AUTHOR

DOCTOR TA SRINIVASEN, is a Corporate Legal Counsel, currently associated with Dalmia Bharat Group, Chennai, India. His earlier associations with various leading Corporates includes the HCL Technologies Group, CavinKare Group, and Dharmsee Parpia Group, in Senior Level Positions for a period spanning over three decades. Wherever associated, as a silent performer he had demonstrated Legal and Secretarial as a function can value add to the core business function for its bottom and topline growth.

Srinivasen, after his Bachelor of Commerce degree from Loyola College, Chennai went on to do his Bachelor of Law degree from Dr. Ambedkar Government Law College, Chennai and thereafter completed his Master's Degree in Law from Annamalai University.

In addition he holds the Master of Business Administration degree from the DoMS of the University of Madras.

He is also the Fellow Member of the Institute of Company Secretaries of India (ICSI) and was elected to become an Associate Member of the Institute of Chartered Secretaries and Administrators, (ICSA) UK.

He was awarded, the Doctor of Philosophy Degree by the University of Madras for his research thesis, *"IPR Management, Protection and Enforcement in India – Need for Stronger IPR Regime"* submitted in the year 2017.

www.ingramcontent.com/pod-product-compliance
Lightning Source LLC
Chambersburg PA
CBHW030841180526
45163CB00004B/1409